Van Haren
PUBLISHING

B C
A
OF ICT

Attitude, Behavior
and Culture of ICT

ABC of ICT

Excercise Workbook

Paul Wilkinson and Jan Schilt

VHP

GamingWorks

Other Publications in the ABC of ICT Series

ABC stands for the Attitude, Behavior and Culture within IT organizations. Use these other great products with your Workbooks to get help and tips for solving worst practices and supporting improvement programs and initiatives within your organization.

ABC of ICT Card Deck

A new approach to dry and formal training and change programs; this card deck makes strong and sound points with a humorous pack of cards.

"Any IT Service Management initiative that doesn't address ABC is bound for failure......."
Maarten Bordewijk, Getronics-PinkRoccade, senior ITIL trainer, Netherlands

"The ABC card exercise was a lot of fun, and put people immediately to work, brainstorming on the worst practices and their consequences, aided by the easily recognizable cartoons.... This is a great aid for people seeking for certification in the different levels and practices of ITSM, whether it is ITIL or ISO 20000 or other good practices."
Alejandro Debenedet, EXIN, Netherlands

ISBN: 978 90 8753 138 6

ABC of ICT: An Introduction

This book describes what ABC (Attitude, Behavior and Culture) of ICT is, why it is important and gives practical cases and examples in dealing with ABC issues. The book contains more than 35 case examples from industry experts and practitioners on what they have done to solve specific ABC issues. The book can be used in combination with the ABC of ICT card set for creating awareness, assessing your own worst practices and taking your first practical steps in solving them.

".... The ABC book is excellent. Its the best explained set of business change tools that I've ever seen (and I've been in the BPR game since 1998). So good, in fact, that I'm going to get our HR department a copy to help with the work I'm doing with them on improving IT professionalism."
Kevin Holland, Programme Head, Service Management and Delivery Directorate, NHS Connecting for Health

ISBN: 978 908753 140 9

ABC of ICT

Exercise Workbook

Van Haren
PUBLISHING

Colophon

Title:	ABC of ICT: The Exercise Workbook
Authors:	Paul Wilkinson and Jan Schilt
Editor:	Steve Newton
Publisher:	Van Haren Publishing, Zaltbommel, www.vanharen.net
ISBN:	978 90 8753 142 3
Print:	First edition, first impression, January 2009
Layout and design:	CO2 Premedia bv, Amersfoort -- NL
Cover design:	Adapted from a design by 02 Creative, Norwich
Copyright:	© 2009 GamingWorks

For any further enquiries about Van Haren Publishing, please send an e-mail to:
info@vanharen.net
Although this publication has been composed with most care, neither Author nor Editor nor Publisher can accept any liability for damage caused by possible errors and/or incompleteness in this publication.

Contents

Foreword

This book, and the ABC of ICT(tm) concept has been developed by Paul Wilkinson and Jan Schilt from GamingWorks BV in the Netherlands.

We are not only the developers of the ABC of ICT(tm) but also the developers of Business Simulations such as Apollo 13 - an ITSM case experience(tm) , The Challenge of Egypt(tm), The Greatest Move(tm), Taikiti Bay(tm) and the Grab@Pizza(tm). Both our Business Simulations and the ABC of ICT(tm) products are based on critical success and fail factors in applying best practices, and didactical principles about learning and development.

During our travels around the world we have met hundreds of managers who have taken part in our Business Simulations. During these simulations they shared their deepest reflections on reasons of failure and the keys factors for success. Triggered by the realistic interactions and environment of the simulations they are the ones who gave us the knowledge and insights to develop the ABC of ICT product set.

With our background in Human Resource Development and our background in ICT organizational change we were able to combine all of these elements to develop this practical and useful set of ABC cards. Use them to 'play' with, and confront your management, if you or they do not believe that ITSM initiatives fail because of ABC, then just play our Apollo 13 - an ITSM case experience(tm). You will experience it for yourselves. We need tell you no more...

Use our ABC of ICT(tm) products in your organization and with your people. Use our workbooks, our exercises and check the website www.abc-of-ict.com for the latest info. The website will identify world wide supplier organizations that have embraced the ABC of ICT(tm) and who will be able to help you. Use the products in your training, consulting and during client sessions. It will bring you and your customer added value. If you need any further help you know where to find us.

Lots of ABC success,

Paul and Jan
GamingWorks

Chapter 1
Introduction to this Workbook

This is an exercise workbook that can be used to facilitate team exercises using the ABC of ICT card set. The ABC of ICT card set is one of a set ABC products aimed at helping organizations improve.

The ABC of ICT card set is an awareness and assessment instrument primarily aimed at creating dialogue and a 'sense-of-urgency' for change.

There is also a sister publication, 'ABC of ICT – An Introduction'. This is a book which contains case studies and practical tips for solving the ABC worst practices identified by performing the exercises in this workbook.

This workbook contains:

- A description of what ABC is and why it is relevant.
- A description of the ABC of ICT card set.
- A number of exercises that can be performed using the ABC of ICT card set.
- Worksheets that can be completed, by the delegates as part of the exercises (the facilitator may copy these worksheets to give to each team or participant as they wish).
- Introduction and reflection notes and teacher tips to assist a facilitator in running the exercises.

The appendices in this workbook contain:

- The global results of the ABC worst practice workshops held at the time of publication. These identify the most commonly chosen ABC worst practices and the impact they cause.
- An example of how 'attitude and behavior' was changed using the ABC cards.
- An example of a follow up initiative for helping to solve an ABC issue. There are more examples of this available in the book 'ABC of ICT – An Introduction', which contains a number of cases from internationally recognized experts, describing what they have done to solve ABC issues.

This workbook can be used stand-alone, together with the ABC of ICT set of cards. There are also separate student manuals that can be obtained. These are particularly relevant and useful when the exercises are being performed as part of a formalized, open ITIL or ABC training. Each student will then have their own manual and can record the results of each of the exercises as well as personal notes and follow-up actions. *If you are not using the student manual as part of your session then please ignore all references in teacher tips which relate to this manual.*

The exercises in this workbook have been carefully chosen to align with some key concepts of IT service management according to ITIL V3, and to match the most significant ABC (Attitude, Behavior, Culture) issues and worst practices that are common to IT organizations. *Worst practices that are preventing IT organizations from realizing the benefits of ITSM best practices such as ITIL.*

The key concepts of IT service management according to ITIL V3 are:

- Service management is a set of specialized organizational capabilities for providing **value** to **customers** in the form of **services.**

- A service is a means of delivering **value** to customers by facilitating **outcomes** that **customers** want to achieve without the ownership of **specific costs** and **risks**.

- Value is defined as:
  - **Utility** is derived from the attributes of the service that have a positive effect on the performance of activities, objects, and tasks associated with desired outcomes. Removal or relaxation of constraints on performance is also perceived as a positive effect.
  - **Warranty** is derived from the positive effect being available when it is needed, in sufficient capacity or magnitude, and dependably in terms of continuity and security.
  - **Utility** is what the customer gets, and **warranty** is how it is delivered.

The are five main exercises in this handbook. These exercises focus on:

- **'Customer and user focused'**
  What is the 'customer' or 'user' perception of our ABC worst practices? What impact and consequences do these have? Are these worst practices viewed as acceptable business risks? Is anybody currently 'responsible' and 'accountable' for resolving these worst practices? This exercise has been chosen because global results show that a common worst practice is 'IT is too internally focused'.

- **'Value'**
  Do we KNOW what value we should be delivering? Does everybody have a shared understanding of that value? Are we currently demonstrating that value? This exercise has been chosen because of the emphasis of ITIL on realizing value, however trend reports show we are still poor at measuring value.

- **'Resistance'**
  What type of resistance will we (or do we) see and experience if we try to apply ITSM best practices? This exercise has been chosen because more than 50% of ITIL initiatives that fail do so because of 'resistance'.

- **'Training and competence needs'**
  Will the current ITIL training and certification help us address the ABC worst practices that we identify in OUR organizations? What training do we need? How do we ensure our partners have the right skills and competences for addressing ABC issues? This exercise has been chosen because results of a mini survey we conducted showed that 94% of the respondents felt that 'current ITIL training and certification does not adequately help address ABC issues'.

- **'Leadership and commitment'**
  Is there real commitment to making change happen, and appropriate leadership to ensure that it does? This exercise has been chosen because one of the key common success and fail factors mentioned by the experts in the 'ABC of ICT: An Introduction' book was leadership and senior level commitment.

The most significant ABC issues and worst practices are represented in the 57 cartoons on the ABC cards. It is worth noting that:

- These are industry recognized worst practices gathered from literally thousands of students who have undergone 'Apollo 13 – an ITSM case experience' business simulation, as well as input from the hundreds of the international training and consulting partners of GamingWorks.

- The results of the evaluations of the students who have played Apollo reveal the largest success and fail factor is related to 'people'. 44.7% declared this to be the most important success or fail factor.

Chapter 2
The ABC of ICT™

What is the ABC of ICT?

ABC of ICT stands for the Attitude, Behavior and Culture within ICT organizations. In the past 10 years or so many IT organizations have adopted 'best practice' frameworks such as ITIL to bring IT under control. However, many of these organizations have failed to realize the expected benefits of such frameworks. **Why is this?** Because of ABC issues. It is our belief that it is the ABC 'worst practices' that will determine the success or failure of your ITSM improvement initiatives, not the frameworks and the models.

**It is ABC that will prevent you from realizing the value offered by these frameworks.
It is ABC that presents a business risk.**

IT is becoming increasingly important to business operations and to all types of businesses. As such we can no longer afford to fail to successfully apply these types of frameworks. It is time we recognized and resolved the ABC worst practices once and for all. It is this need to bring IT under control that has partly led to the rise of IT governance. A Weill & Ross investigation into IT governance, described it as follows:

Specifying the decision rights and accountability framework

to

encourage the desirable behavior in the use of IT

We in IT have focused for too long now on the first part, the *'frameworks'*, and not enough on the second part - the *'desirable behavior'*. This is why many IT improvement initiatives fail.

A Forrester report revealed that **52%** fail because of 'resistance to change' (Attitude). A further 29% fail because of a lack of business interest or involvement (Attitude). Findings from our own 'Apollo 13 – an ITSM case experience' business simulation (see the article *'Using simulations to* *increase the success of your ITSM initiative'* published in the IT Service Management Global Best Practice book – volume 1, 2008, Van Haren Publishing) also reveal that the key learning point, identified by more than 1,000 students is that **'People related issues'** are the most significant success or fail factor in improving IT performance. Issues such as the need for:

- clearly defined, agreed and accepted tasks, roles and responsibilities;
- personal accountability;
- creating buy-in and commitment;
- leading change and 'walking-the-talk';
- 'acting' customer focused instead of 'saying we are' customer focused;
- breaking down organizational 'silos';
- managing the soft issues relating to organizational change.

A description of A, B and C

'Attitude'

This is what people think and feel. It is their demeanour and how they react to the world about them. How they react to a change initiative, a colleague or a customer. Examples of attitude are:

- Somebody thinking "The users are ALWAYS complaining....just ignore them they will soon go away!"
- Somebody thinking "...I'll believe that when I see it..." after a manager has just announced 100% commitment to the ITIL program.

'Behavior'

This is what people do. Behavior is influenced by attitude and by the culture of the organization. Examples of behavior are:

- Somebody saying they will follow the ITIL procedures but not doing it.
- Not registering a resolution, or not transferring knowledge to a first line employee even though you know it would help, and even knowing you should be doing it.

'Culture'

This can be described as the accepted ways of working within an organization, the values and standards that people find as normal. Examples of culture are:

- 'Knowledge is power', or the 'hero culture', where people believe that sharing knowledge diminishes their own value, therefore they want to be the only ones with the expertise and knowledge, ensuring that they are the heroes.
- The blame culture - everybody points the finger of blame and mistakes are punished.

In fact you could say that 'Attitude' is individual and comes as a result of personal beliefs and experiences which influence behavior. Culture is often difficult to grasp but could be described as the corporate attitude. Often employees in an organization are unaware of the culture and how this influences their personal attitude and behavior. This is why culture is one of the most difficult things to change. It is 'soft', you can't see it, you can't touch it, you know it's there, you can get bogged down in it and unable to move, it can stop a change program in its tracks. It is something to be taken seriously if you want your change program to succeed.....it would seem that the most common approach is to ignore it and hope that it will go away or change by itself.

What are the current solutions?

Unfortunately neither existing frameworks and 'best practice' guidance, certification programs, conference sessions or articles adequately tell you how to address these issues. Things are slowly improving as more providers finally understand the need to address the 'management of change' aspects involved when deploying ITSM frameworks and methods.

A new certification scheme and a set of offerings are being launched as part of ITIL V3 certification. As yet it is unknown to what degree these offerings will address ABC issues.

In the Netherlands the itSMF have now devoted a complete conference stream to ABC.

The exercises in this book and the ABC card set are intended to help IT organizations address these ABC issues.

The ABC of ICT card set is part of a range of ABC products aimed at helping organizations improve. There is also a sister publication 'ABC of ICT – An Introduction'. This book, published by Van Haren Publishing, contains case studies and practical tips for solving the ABC worst practices. The case studies and tips are given by recognized industry experts and authorities, and include authors from the ITIL V1, ITIL V2 and ITIL V3 publications.

'Apollo 13 – an ITSM case experience' business simulation is an instrument that can be used as a follow up to the exercises, to let people see, feel and experience the success and fail factors actually working, and to learn how to apply their own solutions for resolving the ABC worst practices.

ABC is like an iceberg, much of it hidden below the surface, and difficult to see, but nevertheless dangerous and capable of inflicting enormous damage.

Chapter 3
The ABC of ICT™ Card Set

The ABC of ICT card set contains 57 worst practice cartoons. These are worst practices that industry experts recognize and agree upon, and these are worst practices that are regularly presented by us at itSMF conferences throughout the World. Whenever we present them, people nod (enthusiastically) in agreement and recognition. (We are a little concerned at the smiling, enthusiastic acknowledgement – it sometimes looks almost like pride "Yes! Yes! That is what we do!")

These presentations often receive top scores as people recognize their relevance and importance. The 'ABC of ICT – An Introduction' book also contains characteristics and symptoms of what to look for in order to help you assess whether a worst practice card really does apply to your organization.

This card set has been designed as an awareness and assessment instrument to help teams, departments and organizations to:

- identify, recognize and agree whether these worst practices apply to their own organization;
- look at worst practices from the perspectives of different stakeholders;
- identify how stakeholders are impacted by a worst practice and identify which stakeholders display which type of worst practices;
- enable teams, possibly comprised of various stakeholders, to get together to discuss the worst practices;
- discuss and agree the consequences and risks of these worst practices;
- recognize and create 'buy-in' to the 'need' to find a solution to resolve them;
- identify stakeholders that need to be involved in solving the worst practices;
- discuss and agree possible solutions to resolve the worst practices;
- provide input to 'continual service improvement' initiatives.

The card set is aimed at creating dialogue and discussion so that these ABC issues can be brought out into the open. Once they are brought out into the open and recognized, action can be taken to address them. *So long as they remain hidden, and so long as we avoid talking about them or discussing them, they will remain a danger that may turn into resistance.* Resistance that will prevent your organization from achieving success and, as a result, pose a risk to the business.

The card suits represent Attitude (Clubs), **Behavior** (Diamonds), Culture (Spades) and **Stakeholders** (Hearts). There are five jokers representing People, Process, Product, Partner and Performance.

What can you do with the cards?

You can use the card set in a number of ways, a number of different settings and with a range of objectives. The following list identifies the most common uses:

- You can use them within traditional ITIL awareness or training sessions to help **identify issues** that need resolving by ITIL, or **identify issues** that need resolving if ITIL is to work!

- You can use them in team meetings for **self reflection** and **assessment**, by asking a team of IT people "If we gave these cards to a user, which ones would they choose as being representative of our IT organization".

- You can use these to undertake a real **survey**, giving them to users and customers and asking them to choose worst practices that apply to THEIR IT department.

- You can use them to **confront people by** selecting cards that are appropriate to your organization and putting them on the table when people display a certain worst practice behavior. You can then discuss why a specific card was put on the table.

- You can give them away as **gifts** to all IT staff in order to **create awareness,** perhaps at the start of an improvement program.

- You can put cartoons on your website to raise awareness of issues, and have people vote on the applicability of a worst practice to YOUR organization, and leave quotes and comments. This helps you **capture input** for improvement programs.

Chapter 4
Exercises with the ABC of ICT™ Card Set

Introduction

The following sections describe the exercises that can be performed using the ABC cards.

There are five main exercises in this workbook. These exercises focus on:

- **'Customer and user focused'**
  What are the 'customer' or 'user' perceptions of our ABC worst practices? What impact and consequences do these have? Are these worst practices an acceptable business risk? Is anybody currently 'responsible' and 'accountable' for resolving these worst practices?
  This exercise has been chosen because global results show that a common worst practice is 'IT is too internally focused'.

- **'Value'**
  Do we KNOW what value we should be delivering? Does everybody have a shared understanding of that value? Are we currently demonstrating that value? This exercise has been chosen because of the emphasis of ITIL on realizing value, however trend reports show we are still poor at measuring value.

- **'Resistance'**
  What type of resistance will we (or do we) see and experience if we try to apply ITSM best practices? This exercise has been chosen as more than 50% of ITIL initiatives that fail do so because of 'resistance'.

- **'Training and competence needs'**
  Will the current ITIL training and certification help us address the ABC worst practices we identify in OUR organizations? What training do we need? How do we ensure our partners have the right skills and competences for addressing ABC issues? This exercise has been chosen because results of a mini survey we conducted showed that 94% of the respondents felt that 'current ITIL training and certification does not adequately help address ABC issues'.

- **'Leadership and commitment'**
  Is there real commitment to making change happen, and appropriate leadership to ensure that it does? This exercise has been chosen because one of the key common success and fail factors mentioned by the experts in the ABC of ICT: An Introduction book was leadership and senior level commitment.

These five exercises are described in detail, with each of the descriptions containing:

- exercise objectives;
- introduction and background information;
- instructions;
- tasks;
- teacher tips;
- worksheets.

It is recommended that the facilitator gathers all of the completed worksheets at the end of the session so that a consolidated report can be produced and sent to the delegates. This will, of course, require administrative work by the facilitator. This consolidated report can also be used as input to a 'service improvement initiative'.

There are a number of other example exercises that can be performed using the cards. These additional exercises are described briefly.

The exercises in this book are by no means the complete set of exercises that can be performed. A number of ITIL Training and Consulting companies have developed their own exercises using the cards. *Feel free to be creative and design your own exercises, to challenge and confront your class.* If you do, then please let us know so that we can add them or share them with others.

Exercise 1 – Customer and user focused

Exercise objectives

The objectives of this exercise are to:

- Identify if the delegates are 'customer and user focused' in terms of their attitude, their behavior and their culture. Our industry surveys reveal between 75% to 89% of IT professionals still feel '*we are NOT customer focused enough*' in IT.
- Identify what the delegates consider 'desirable' or 'undesirable' behavior in relation to 'customer and user focused'.
- Let the delegates identify any ABC worst practices within their own organization, as seen and experienced from a 'customer and user' perspective.
- Let the delegates identify the consequences and risks of any worst practices in relation to ITIL V3 'value'.
- Let the delegates identify if there is anybody responsible or accountable for, or any initiatives for solving these ABC worst practices within their own organization.
- Let the delegates identify which ITIL core activities or processes can help solve the ABC worst practices, enabling them to translate the theory learnt in ITIL training into a practical application within their own organizational context (this is only an objective if ITIL V3 is an important reason for performing the exercise, for example if used as part of a formal ITIL V3 training program).
- Let the delegates gather input for a service improvement program within their own organization.

Exercise background

This exercise was developed because we in IT are still poor at delivering services that meet customer needs, and also because we are still not really 'customer and user focused'.

How can we say this? We have conducted a number of international surveys within itSMF workshops and via websites. We allow people to vote on the statement: 'We are not customer focused enough in IT'. The results of this type of survey show that between 75% and 89% agree!

This exercise is also useful in helping to address one of the top three most commonly chosen worst practices. 'We are still too internally focused in IT'. This exercise forces delegates to think from the user perspective. Another of the top three most commonly chosen worst practices is 'Too little understanding of business impact and priority'. This exercises forces delegates to consider the impact and risks associated with worst practices identified during this exercise.

We have had ITIL and best practice frameworks for more than ten years. The requirement ten years ago from the business was: 'Improve the quality of products and services and be more customer focused'. Ten years later research in the Netherlands revealed the number one strategic issue for IT organizations was?.......The same as ten years ago!

Before starting the exercise ask the delegates the following question

Question: 'What RIGHT does an IT organization have to exist?', 'Why are we here?'.

Stimulate feedback from the delegates. They may respond with: 'Serve the business', 'Guarantee availability of technology', 'Deliver service quality'.

Try to ask reflective questions such as:

- Who is 'the business'?
- Availability to who?
- Service quality to who?

Try to lead them to the following conclusions. Our RIGHT to exist is:

- To support and enable customers and users of IT through the provision of services.
- To fulfil agreements with the customers in terms of 'value' (results achieved) or managing risk (by ensuring availability and continuity of business operations)

Carry out the exercise

Introduce the first exercise

"So if our right to exist is 'meet the needs of customers and users', let's do the first exercise. This is the **'customer and user focused exercise'** to determine if we really are customer focused enough in IT."

Exercise instructions

- Create a small team of four to seven players (or a number of small teams).
- Identify somebody in the group to be the team leader. Somebody who can, and is prepared to document 'legibly' the findings of the group, somebody prepared to present the teams' findings to the room.
- Ensure that somebody in the team manages the time.
- Perform the following team exercise using a minimum of one pack of cards, (preferably each delegate will receive their own set of cards).
- Place the **USER** stakeholder card in the middle of the table (**2 of Hearts**).
- Place the **2 of Clubs** on the table.
- Have the team leader read out the following to the team "*We have had ITIL for more than 20 years. ITIL was all about the users and the customers, and providing services that deliver quality to these users and customers. In a recent mini-survey on the itSMF site in the Netherlands this cartoon was published (2 of Clubs) with a statement. 'We are not customer focused enough in IT'. You would expect after 20 years of ITIL that this was a ridiculous survey to place there, as this is obviously no longer true. However 89% of respondents AGREED with the statement!*"

Exercise 1: Task 1 – The Vote (10 minutes)

Ask each individual if they agree or disagree with the following statement:

'We are not customer focused enough in IT'.

Exercise 1 – Customer and user focused

Worksheet Task 1: The Vote

Record the answers on this form. Those who agree must give one example of behavior they have seen that supports this; those who disagree can also give one example. Which stakeholder displays this behavior?

	Number of answers
Agree	
Disagree	

Agree comments:

Disagree comments:

Exercise 1 – Customer and user focused

Teacher hints and tips for Exercise 1: Task 1

- Walk around and listen to the discussions and the examples given. Ask the delegates to be 'specific' in naming an **Attitude** or **Behavior** and the associated stakeholder who displays this.
- Ask them to describe something you would see if you were to walk around in their organization.
- If there are multiple stakeholders in the team, you could ask each delegate to take out a stakeholder card (Hearts) that represents their own role and place this in front of themselves on the table. Ask them to give examples from their own role.
- If you hear 'we' or 'they', ask for specifics. For example, if somebody says, when describing customer and user focused behavior: "We ask about and understand business impact". Ask them "Who is 'we'? The help desk? The specialists?" Show them the stakeholder cards and let them choose.
- The examples recorded will help us to identify what the delegates see and experience as 'customer or user focused' behavior, in other words what people themselves find acceptable and non-acceptable behavior. This will also help to identify behavior related to various stakeholders.
- By identifying WHO displays undesirable behavior, we can assign 'ownership' and 'responsibility' for doing something about it. So long as it remains 'WE' nobody feels accountable or responsible.
- Before performing Task 2 you may decide to discuss the results:
  - does everybody agree what is 'desirable' and 'undesirable behavior'?
  - what does 'enough' mean in the statement and how do you decide what 'enough' is?
- If the students each have a student manual (a separate product that can be obtained through GamingWorks, which is particularly relevant and useful when the exercises are being performed as part of a formalized or open ITIL training with students from different organizations), then refer them to the 'personal notes and actions' for Task 1 in their own manual. They can carry out the actions in their own organization.

Exercise 1 – Customer and user focused

Exercise 1: Task 2 - The "user" experience: (10 minutes)

Place the 2 of Hearts prominently in the middle of the table.

Read out the following to the team:

"Imagine if we give the user the ABC cards, which three cards would he or she choose that most typically represent the ABC worst practices in your organization?"

- Let each person choose three. **They may choose the same cards,** they do not have to choose different cards.
- If there is only one set of cards, spread the cards out on the table so that each delegate can see all the cards.
- Let them record their choices by ticking against the appropriate card on the Worksheet for Task 2.

Exercise 1 – Customer and user focused

Worksheet Task 2: The 'user' experience

Each time a card is chosen place a '✓' in the column 'No of times chosen'.

Card	Suit	Description	No of times chosen
2	♣	No respect for, or understanding of users	
3	♣	Knowledge is power	
4	♣	IT not seen as an added value partner to the business	
5	♣	Neither partner makes an effort to understand the other	
6	♣	ITIL never work here	
7	♣	My TOOL will solve ALL your ITSM problems	
8	♣	IT thinks it doesn't need to understand the business to make a business case	
9	♣	Walking the talk	
10	♣	No respect for, or trust in management	
J	♣	Let's outsource the business – we'd be better off	
Q	♣	No understanding of business impact & priority	
K	♣	ITIL is the objective,... not what it should achieve	
A	♣	ITIL certification means I know what I am doing	

Card	Suit	Description	No of times chosen
2	♦	We don't measure our value contribution to strategy	
3	♦	Too little business involvement in requirements specification & testing	
4	♦	Not capturing the right knowledge for reuse	
5	♦	No management commitment	
6	♦	Everything has the highest priority....according to the users	
7	♦	Throwing solutions (ITIL) over the wall and HOPING people will use them	
8	♦	We're going to INSTALL ITIL....it can't be that hard	
9	♦	Maybe we should have tested that change first	
10	♦	Never mind about following procedures....just do what we usually do	
J	♦	Saying **yes** but meaning **no**	
Q	♦	The solution the customer sees isn't the one that IT sees	
K	♦	IT strategy's contribution to business strategy	
A	♦	Process managers without authority	

Exercise 1 – Customer and user focused

Worksheet Task 2: The 'user' experience

Each time a card is chosen place a '✓' in the column 'No of times chosen'.

Card	Suit	Description	No of times chosen
2	♠	Them and Us culture—opposing and competing forces	
3	♠	Hierarchic culture 'The boss is always right, even when the boss is wrong!'	
4	♠	Internally focused	
5	♠	Punishment culture	
6	♠	Hero culture	
7	♠	9 to 5 culture	
8	♠	Plan, Do, stop….no real continual improvement culture	
9	♠	Promotion on ability	
10	♠	The superiority complex 'We know best!'	
J	♠	Avoidance culture	
Q	♠	Not my responsibility	
K	♠	Empowering people	
A	♠	Blame culture	

Card	Suit	Description	No of times chosen
2	♥	The user...creature at the end of the evolutionary chain	
3	♥	The help desk technoid...Hello HELPLESS desk....what do you want NOW?	
4	♥	The IT manager. The best way to improve services is to outsource...the business!	
5	♥	The consultant...without me the world will stop spinning	
6	♥	The technogeek...That problem isn't in my book, therefore it doesn't exist	
7	♥	Business manager...Demand & Give. I demand and you give in	
8	♥	The CIO...The buck stops anywhere but here!	
9	♥	The supplier...OK so the functionality isn't great but look at the flashy interface!	
10	♥	The quality manager...waiting for the IT organization to improve	
J	♥	The ITIL consultant...A process flow and some procedures are all you need	
Q	♥	The project manager...Of course we will finish on time and within budget	
K	♥	The CEO...Which part of NO didn't you understand	
A	♥	HRD manager...our IT staff are now strategic assets?	
	Joker	...The Silo mentality (Process)	
	Joker	Outsourcing saves costs....whilst maintaining quality (Partner)	
	Joker	A tool solves all problems (Product)	
	Joker	Unable to specify the VALUE required by the business (Performance)	
	Joker	IT as a business enabler and differentiator (People)	

Exercise 1 – Customer and user focused

Teacher hints and tips for Exercise 1: Task 2

- Walk around and explain to the team why they are performing this exercise. Explain that one of the top three most common worst practices is that '*IT is too internally focused*'. Explain that this is aimed at forcing them to think like a user.
- Remind the team that more than one person can choose the same card, they do not all have to choose three different cards.
- Prompt the team to record the choices made by ticking the worksheets.
- Gather these worksheets in afterwards to enable you to prepare a consolidated report.
- Please send the results of these worksheets to office@gamingworks.nl. GamingWorks will consolidate all results into a global trend sheet and make this available to all ABC of ICT users.

Exercise 1 – Customer and user focused

Exercise 1: Task 3 - Impact, consequences and risks (15 minutes)

Firstly, explain to the team the following. 'You have now simply identified a set of worst practices you believe YOUR users would choose. However nobody really feels any 'need' or 'urgency' for doing anything about these. We will now undertake the next task. In this task you, as a team, must now choose the team top 3.' (or 1 depending upon time constraints).

Ask the team first "How will you decide a top three?" They may decide that the card chosen the most is the top card. Ask them to choose the top three based upon '**impact, consequences and potential business risk.**'

Explain the following ITIL V3 theory:

- Service management is a set of specialized organizational capabilities for providing **value** to **customers** in the form of **services**.
- Services are a means of delivering **value** to customers by facilitating the **outcomes** that customers want to achieve without the ownership of specific **costs** and **risks**.
- Value is defined as:
- **Utility** – the attributes of the service that have a positive effect on the performance that is associated with desired outcomes. Removal or relaxation of constraints on performance is also perceived as a positive effect.
- **Warranty** - the positive effect being available when it is needed, in sufficient capacity or magnitude, and dependably in terms of continuity and security.

ITIL V3 focuses on **value**, delivering **outcomes**, realizing **performance gains,** as well as **minimizing risks and costs**.

'Choose the top three based upon the negative impact and consequences on value, i.e. outcomes not achieved, delays in deployment, revenue lost, wrong investment decisions, downtime, rework, threats to continuity, additional costs. When the impact is known, discuss whether this is an acceptable business risk.'

- Write down a brief example of the behavior seen that supports the choice, and the stakeholder who displays this behavior.
- Write down the consequences of this behavior in the form of a few key bullet points.
- Discuss the consequences and whether these top three ABC issues are acceptable risks for the team, and for the business. Document your views.
- If anybody in your team has had experience in successfully resolving one of the top three worst practices, ask them to describe how.

Card:	Symptoms: *Describe an example of behavior you have seen that is related to the card, also the stakeholders who display this behavior.*	Consequences: *What are consequences, in terms of customer satisfaction, costs, downtime, delays.*	Acceptable risk?
Example: 3 ♣ Knowledge is power	• Specialists didn't explain how to solve common production failures to ops. • Specialists didn't record solution in tool	• Increased down time • Production system delayed • Wasted time and costs seeking solution • Dissatisfied customer • Dissatisfied ops	Not for supporting critical production systems

Exercise 1 – Customer and user focused

Teacher hints and tips for Exercise 1: Task 3

- This is an important task. This is where the team is creating value. Simply identifying a set of worst practice cards has no association with impact and consequences, and does not create a 'need' or 'sense of urgency' for resolving.
- Explain to the team why we are doing this exercise. One of the most common worst practices chosen is 'No understanding of business impact and priority', and we are now forcing the team to consider the impact of worst practices THEY THEMSELVES HAVE IDENTIFIED.
- The teams often are so busy discussing and discovering that they forget to record. Walk around and prompt them to record a real life set of behaviors they have observed, and encourage them to record the impact and consequences. As soon as they have identified a card together with the associated symptoms and consequences, get them to discuss and record whether this poses an acceptable business risk.
- Some delegates may not agree with their team's top three. If this happens let the student(s) choose their own personal number one and add this to the list so that you have maybe four or five examples. It is important that everybody identifies with the worst practices chosen as being relevant to their organization.
- Some teams may not be able to make the step towards analysing behavior in relation to the business. If this is so, ask them to record the consequences to the IT organization. When they have done this make the link to the business, if possible, in your role as facilitator:

Example: card chosen 3 of Clubs 'Knowledge is power'. They may say the consequences are "Help desk doesn't learn how to resolve incidents". If so, ask them "What does that then mean to the business?" For example, it may take longer to solve, the user is non-productive for longer, or not able to perform an important business activity. This causes increased down time, non availability and, depending upon the seriousness, may also result in loss of revenue.

It is important that the team is confronted with and discovers the impact of worst practices on the business, so that they can learn why the service strategy concept of 'value' is of importance to EVERYBODY in IT, not just IT directors and managers.

You could also explain as additional supporting evidence:

ISO20000: **Requirements for a management system**

Competence, Awareness & Training

- Top management SHALL ensure that its employees are aware of the relevance and importance of their activities and how they contribute to results.

If anybody in the team has resolved one of the worst practices then ask them to explain how. Who managed this? How did they change the attitude of people? How did they ensure new behavior was carried out and consistent? They may be able to offer some practical tips for other delegates.

Exercise 1 – Customer and user focused

Worksheet Task 3: Impact, consequences and risks

Card:	Symptoms: Describe an example of behavior you have seen that is related to the card, also the stakeholders who display this behavior.	Consequences: What are consequences, in terms of customer satisfaction, costs, downtime, delays.	Acceptable risk?
		Poor IT investment decisions ❑ Lost business opportunities ❑ Lost revenue ❑ Damaged business reputation ❑ Decreased staff productivity ❑ Higher business operating costs ❑ Failure to comply with regulations ❑ Other ❑ Higher IT costs ❑ Increased downtime ❑ Dissatisfied customers ❑ Delays in deploying IT solutions ❑ Solutions don't meet business needs ❑ Unreliable service quality ❑ Threats to business continuity ❑ Other ❑	
		Poor IT investment decisions ❑ Lost business opportunities ❑ Lost revenue ❑ Damaged business reputation ❑ Decreased staff productivity ❑ Higher business operating costs ❑ Failure to comply with regulations ❑ Other ❑ Higher IT costs ❑ Increased downtime ❑ Dissatisfied customers ❑ Delays in deploying IT solutions ❑ Solutions don't meet business needs ❑ Unreliable service quality ❑ Threats to business continuity ❑ Other ❑	

Exercise 1 – Customer and user focused

Worksheet Task 3: Impact, consequences and risks

Card:	Symptoms: Describe an example of behavior you have seen that is related to the card, also the stakeholders who display this behavior.	Consequences: What are consequences, in terms of customer satisfaction, costs, downtime, delays.	Acceptable risk?
		Poor IT investment decisions ❑ Lost business opportunities ❑ Lost revenue ❑ Damaged business reputation ❑ Decreased staff productivity ❑ Higher business operating costs ❑ Failure to comply with regulations ❑ Other ❑ Higher IT costs ❑ Increased downtime ❑ Dissatisfied customers ❑ Delays in deploying IT solutions ❑ Solutions don't meet business needs ❑ Unreliable service quality ❑ Threats to business continuity ❑ Other ❑	
		Poor IT investment decisions ❑ Lost business opportunities ❑ Lost revenue ❑ Damaged business reputation ❑ Decreased staff productivity ❑ Higher business operating costs ❑ Failure to comply with regulations ❑ Other ❑ Higher IT costs ❑ Increased downtime ❑ Dissatisfied customers ❑ Delays in deploying IT solutions ❑ Solutions don't meet business needs ❑ Unreliable service quality ❑ Threats to business continuity ❑ Other ❑	

Exercise 1 – Customer and user focused

Exercise 1: Task 4 - presentation: (5 minutes – each team)

Present the teams' findings:

- How many people agreed with the statement:
  '**We are not customer focused enough in IT**'.
- What were the top three worst practices?
- For the top worst practice chosen, describe an example of behavior, consequence and risks.

Discuss the following (allowing 10 minutes) for one team's results:

- Which worst practices pose an unacceptable business risk?
- Now ask the most important question: 'Is anybody currently responsible and accountable for solving these worst practices?' Very often the answer to this is NO. Explain to the group that so far the TOP chosen worst practice is '*Not my responsibility*'.
- Are there any projects currently actively focused on:
  - People (TRR (Tasks, Roles and Responsibilities), training, skills development);
  - Process (design and deployment);
  - Product (management tool selection/deployment);
  - Partner (partner selection, negotiation or agreements);
  - Performance (defining, monitoring, measuring, reporting on performance).
- If so, will these projects address these worst practices? Are they aimed at mitigating the risks associated with the identified worst practices?
- Explain how the above represents the 4 P's of service design, with the addition of a 5th P, representing 'Performance' or 'Value' in fact. Value being the objective of the initiatives according Service Strategy.
- If not, what can be done to mitigate these risks?
- Explain to the team that they could develop a proposal for their own organization. The proposal might contain:
  - identified worst practice;
  - concrete examples of behavior;
  - identified impact, consequences and risk;
  - current ownership and projects for resolving;
  - proposed 'risk' mitigation initiatives;
  - indication of value or outcomes that can be improved.
- If this is part of a formalized training class then explain to the team that they could do this exercise themselves back in their own organizations, departments or teams.
- If the intention is to run Task 5 (ITIL V3) then the results of this task are now used as input to Task 5. The 'risk' mitigation initiatives can be coupled to ITIL V3.
- If the students each have a student manual, then refer them to the 'personal notes and actions' for Task 4 in their own manual. They can perform these actions back in their own organization.

Exercise 1 – Customer & user focused

Exercise instructions: ITIL V3

If the organization is currently considering, or is already active with ITIL V3, or this exercise is being performed as part of an ITIL V3 training program, you can perform the following additional task.

This task will help to determine the level of understanding of ITIL V3 theory. Can the team identify the core ITIL V3 aspects that can be used to resolve the worst practices identified in Task 4?

Exercise 1: Task 5 – ITIL V3 solutions: (20 minutes)

Identify which ITIL V3 processes or activities are 'core' to resolving these worst practices:

- Ask the team to choose their top worst practice card.
- Record the card chosen and describe the ITIL V3 book and related process, activity and function that will help resolve the identified worst practice.

Card:	ITIL V3 'core' process	
Example: 2 ♦ We don't measure our value contribution to strategy		

Card:	ITIL V3 'core' process	
Example: 2 ♦ We don't measure our value contribution to strategy	Service Strategy: • Service Portfolio Management (Services in terms of Business Value) Service Design: • Measurements Design Continual Service Improvement: • 7 Step Improvement Approach • Service Measurement • Service Reporting	

Exercise 1 – Customer & User focused

Worksheet Task 5: ITIL V3 solutions

Card:	ITIL V3 'core' process, activity, function

Exercise 1 – Customer and user focused

Teacher hints and tips for Exercise 1: Task 5

- In order to perform this task effectively, the facilitator must know ITIL V3 well enough to be able to help and discuss with the team which core elements of ITIL V3 address each ABC card.
- Let the students go through their ITIL V3 training material if these exercises are being performed as part of an ITIL training class.
- If the ITIL V3 books are available, then let the teams use these books. It will help them familiarize themselves with the content.
- It may be that multiple processes might be viewed as a solution to a particular card. If this happens, discuss it and explain that there is no correct answer. Discuss why a particular process was chosen.
- Discuss how the delegates can use this information to help provide input to a service improvement proposal, specifying ITIL as risk mitigation for the identified worst practices from Task 4.
- *GamingWorks have developed a document that matches each ABC card to specific ITIL V3 content. This material can be obtained through licence from GamingWorks.*
- If the students each have a student manual, then refer them to the 'personal notes and actions' for Task 5 in their own manual. They can perform these actions back in their own organization.
- Explain to the students that what they have done so far is, in fact, a continual service improvement (CSI) initiative. They have recognized a weakness, matched it to the impact (negative) on VALUE and have now identified ITIL aspects that can be used to improve value. The team could now document this and present it to their management.

Exercise 2 – Value

Exercise objectives

The objectives of this exercise are to:

- Raise awareness for the ITIL V3 concepts of 'value'.
- Identify if the delegates KNOW the value they NEED to deliver to the business.
- Identify if this is a common, shared knowledge if the group are from the same company.
- Identify if this is something they KNOW or ASSUME.
- Identify whether there is documented evidence to support this.
- Identify whether IT is monitoring, measuring and demonstrating achievement of this value.
- Overcome a number of the most commonly chosen ABC worst practice cards, in particular 'IT is too internally focused' and 'We do not measure our value contribution to strategy'.

Exercise background

This exercise was developed because we in IT are still poor at measuring and demonstrating value to the business.

How can we say this? A recent Parity report revealed *'Only 27% of IT managers have directly measured the return on investment from ITIL implementations, and under half measured the value that IT service management delivered to their business.'*

We used the cards in a workshop at the itSMF Best Practice conference. More than 60 delegates were asked to name the top three worst practice cards that THEIR users would choose in relation to THEIR IT organization.

The TOP scoring worst practice card was: 'We don't measure our value contribution to strategy'.

The results of a poll conducted on the Van Haren website, using the ABC cards revealed the following:

> **Poll**: "*The senior business management in my organization **understand and act** on our IT metrics reports*"

72% disagreed and **28%** agreed.

Before you can start to deliver value you need to know WHAT THAT VALUE is.

The Apollo 13 business simulation has been played by thousands of IT employees. Our research indicates that more than 90% of IT employees don't KNOW what value they should be delivering to the business.

Before starting the exercise, ask the students 'What is value?'

Remind the delegates of the following:

- Value is defined as:
  Utility – the attributes of the service that have a positive effect on the performance that is associated with desired outcomes. Removal or relaxation of constraints on performance is also perceived as a positive effect.
  Warranty - the positive effect being available when it is needed, in sufficient capacity or magnitude, and dependably in terms of continuity and security.

Exercise instructions

- Place the Value Joker on the table
- Read the following to the team:

Imaging now the CEO is sitting opposite you. He says '*So you are spending all this IT budget on improving ITSM to add **VALUE** to MY business. Do you **KNOW** what VALUE I **need** you to deliver?*'

Carry out the exercise

Exercise 2: Task 1 – KPI's

Conduct the following exercise individually (5 minutes):

- Write down for yourself a key performance indicator (KPI) that will demonstrate that you are delivering VALUE. Use the worksheet provided.
- If we visit your organization, could you SHOW us where this is documented?
- Do YOUR IT reports demonstrate achievement of this VALUE?

Exercise 2 – Value

Teacher hints and tips for Exercise 2: Task 1

- If the teams are struggling to identify what value is because they are too far removed from the business, try to help them identify at a high abstraction level what the business demands the MOST from IT. For example, is IT being asked to:
  - lower costs or keep costs under control;
  - deliver high availability of services, guaranteeing continuity of critical information systems;
  - deliver faster and more reliable new information systems and solutions;
  - meet customer satisfaction levels;
  - ensure processes can be audited for compliance.
- If they are struggling, ask them what type of presentations and plans they see from IT directors and what type of key messages are in those presentations. For example, 'Achieving operational excellence', 'Doing more with less', 'Keeping the business running'. These are titles of IT director presentations that reveal a need to either manage costs, or deliver availability and continuity.
- If the teams are struggling, ask them what types of targets and statistics get reported, or what types do their department need to deliver?
- If the teams do not know ask them "Do you think you should know? Or is it not necessary for your role?"

Exercise 2 – Value

Worksheet Task 1: KPI's

Example:

KPI	Description	
Demonstrate compliance to regulations	• To be able to guarantee business continuity demands. • To be able to guarantee integrity and confidentiality of business information. • To ensure that the business passes compliancy controlsin order to demonstrate 'control' to the shareholders. (e.g. Sarbanes Oxley)	

KPI	Description	

Exercise 2 – Value

Exercise 2: Task 2 – Understanding value

Discuss the results (5 minutes):

- Does everybody know the VALUE they need to deliver?
- Does the team feel they SHOULD know, or do they feel it is not necessary for their role?
- If not, how can you demonstrate achievement if most people don't KNOW what value they should be delivering. **What do the auditors say?**

ISO20000: Monitoring, Measuring & Reviewing

- The organization SHALL apply suitable methods for monitoring and, where applicable, measurement of the service management processes. These methods SHALL demonstrate the ability to achieve planned results.

CobiT: ME1 Monitor and Evaluate IT Performance
Management of the process of *'monitor and evaluate IT performance'* that satisfies the business requirement for IT of *transparency and understanding of IT cost, benefits, strategy, policies and service levels in accordance with governance.*

ISO20000: Requirements for a management system

- Top management SHALL ensure that its employees are aware of the relevance and importance of their activities and how they **contribute to results**.

NEN-ISO/IEC 38500:2008 Corporate Governance of Information Technology includes PERFORMANCE as one of the key principles.

Now is the time to ENSURE that the whole IT organization KNOWS what the VALUE needs to be, and that ITSM processes can actually measure, AND demonstrate that VALUE.

- Does top management ensure that the goals are known to all?
- Does top management ensure that employees are aware of the relevance and importance of their activities and how they CONTRIBUTE TO RESULTS?
- If the answers to the above two points are 'NO', what is your responsibility? What should YOU do?

Exercise 2: Task 3 - presentation

Present the findings (3 minutes per team):

- Do we ALL KNOW what VALUE we should be delivering?
- What should WE all be doing to ensure that we KNOW?

Exercise 2 – Value

Teacher hints and tips for Exercise 2: Task 3

- If the delegates are currently engaged in, or considering, an ITIL deployment then you can tell them to capture the responses and use them as input to a service improvement program. They can ensure that 'awareness' and 'communication' sessions clarify the reasons for, and results to be delivered by, the ITIL deployment.
- If the students each have a student manual then refer them to the 'personal notes and actions' for Task 5 in their own manual. They can perform these actions back in their own organization.

Exercise 3 – Resistance

Exercise objectives

The objectives of this exercise are to:

- Identify the types of resistance delegates expect to see, or actually see in relation to ITSM or ITIL improvement initiatives within their organization.
- Let the delegates identify their own personal resistance to an ITSM or ITIL change program.
- Enable those responsible for ITIL improvement initiatives to identify the types of resistance that they will need to address.

Exercise background

A recent Forrester report revealed that the most common reason for this type of project to fail is '52% resistance to change'.

Very often people are 'SENT' or 'TOLD TO GO' on ITIL training. Very often delegates are suspicious of ITIL and do not believe it will help. Often there is no buy-in, or insufficient management commitment to ensuring the improvements are embedded in the behavior and culture of the organization.

Before starting with the exercise ask the delegates the following

Question: 'Are you currently busy with an ITIL or ITSM improvement program or will you be starting one?' 'What is the reason that you are on this training course or attending this workshop?'

Write down the answers, if people do not know or care this is also a possible symptom of 'resistance'.

Carry out the exercise

Exercise 3: Task 1 – Identifying resistance: (10 minutes)

Identify resistance to ITSM improvement initiatives within YOUR organization.?

- Read the following statement to the team: *A Forrester report revealed that the biggest reason for ITSM improvement programs failing is that 52% of stakeholders are resistant to change'*
- Select the cards that most closely represent the type of resistance you would EXPECT, or already SEE and EXPERIENCE in your organization.
- Which card most closely represents your personal resistance to an ITSM or ITIL initiative within YOUR organization.
- Which stakeholders are guilty of this type of resistance?
- Give a concrete example.
- Which stakeholders need to resolve this?

Exercise 3 – Resistance

Worksheet Task 1: Identifying resistance

Example:

Card	Example	Expected(E) Seen(S) Own personal (P)	Stakeholder to resolve
3 ♣ Knowledge is power	• Second line staff refuse to update incident resolution or spend time explaining.	S	Line manager must enforce

Card	Example	Expected(E) Seen(S) Own personal(P)	Stakeholder to resolve

Card	Example	Expected(E) Seen(S) Own personal(P)	Stakeholder to resolve

Exercise 3 – Resistance

Exercise 3: Task 2 – Discussion: (10 minutes)

Discuss the various findings:

- What are the most common examples chosen?
- What do we think are the reasons for this resistance? Are there any relationships between the cards?
- What are the 'personal' forms of resistance? Are people prepared to talk openly about these?
- Has anybody overcome this type of resistance? If so, encourage them to explain how this was achieved.
- If the students each have a student manual then refer them to the 'personal notes and actions' for Task 2 in their own manual. They can perform these actions back in their own organization.

Exercise 3 – Resistance

Teacher hints and tips for Exercise 3: Task 1:

- Rosabeth Moss Kanter identified 10 reasons why people resist change. These are documented in the Service Transition book (5.2.10.4) and can be summarized as follows:
  - **Loss of control** – if you move people from a process or function with which they are familiar to one they know little about, they will experience a feeling of losing control;
  - **Excessive personal uncertainty** – the first question most people will ask is "What is this going to mean for me and for my job?";
  - **Avoid surprises** – people like to be given the opportunity and the time to think through the implications of change for them. Springing new ideas on people may create resistance;
  - **The difference effect** – people build identities around many aspects of their work – their role, the job, the office environment, the company name or logo – it gives them a sense of tradition (this is what people often call the 'culture' of the organization);
  - **Loss of face** – people dislike moving from a position in which they are skilled and competent to one in which they are a novice and must learn. This can often happen when new processes and ways of working are introduced;
  - **Fear around competence** – some people will believe that they cannot adapt to the new ways of working or the new responsibilities: "You can't teach an old dog new tricks!", or "Promoting somebody above their competence and comfort";
  - **Ripples** – the unexpected effect that an action taken in one area has upon another. Managers would be naïve to think that a planned change is trouble-free; sometimes it is impossible to predict accurately the effect one change will have on another part of the organization;
  - **Increase in workload** – change frequently results in more work;
  - **Past resentments** – if the proposed change is associated with an individual, team or organization about which the person has a history of grievance, they may resist the change, even if they consider it a good idea;
  - **Real threats** – there are times when change is going to have a negative impact on the individual, and they are justified in resisting. Pretending it is going to be all right does not help.
- Use the above as part of the discussions.
- Make notes on a flip-chart of all the feedback.
- If people did not know, or care why they were sent on the training, discuss this. Did they ask their managers why they should attend, and what was expected of them?
- Capture the findings and use these as input to any 'service improvement initiative that is current or planned'. Also if you are going to facilitate the 'commitment and leadership' exercise, use the results and findings from this exercise as input, especially if any of the chosen cards and feedback relates to management.
- See Appendix C for an example follow-up intervention aimed at overcoming resistance and creating buy-in for adopting ITSM best practices.

Exercise 4 – Training needs

Exercise objectives

The objectives of this exercise are to:

- Identify whether the current ITIL training enables the delegates to address the ABC issues they have identified in their own organization.
- To use the input from other exercises to confront managers and process owners with the types of issues they need to resolve.
- Identify whether managers and process owners feel they have the right skills and capabilities for solving these ABC issues.

Exercise background

A recent Forrester report revealed that the most common reason for this type of project to fail is '52% of stakeholders are resistant to change'. Current ITIL training and certification is focused on ITIL process expertise and NOT on changing Attitude, Behavior or Culture. In a recent survey we conducted using the cards, 94% agreed to the statement 'Current ITIL training and certification does not adequately address ABC'.

Before starting with the exercise remind the team the following:

- Service management is a set of **specialized organizational capabilities** for providing **value** to **customers** in the form of **services.**
- Either we must develop these capabilities through training and competence development, or we must buy these capabilities in until we are capable ourselves.

Exercise 4 – Training needs

Exercise introduction

- Carry out THIS exercise after you have already identified, using the ABC cards, which worst practices apply to YOUR organization.
- Place the Ace of Clubs card on the table.
- Read out the following to the team:
  - "The current *ITIL V3 certification scheme is all about obtaining 22 points. Following a series of bridging classes and foundation type exams aimed at 'certification' will give you 22 points and allow you to declare yourself ITIL V3 certified.*
  - *A new set of ITIL 'practitioner' level training is being developed, but it is not yet known whether this will address the ABC issues.*
  - *The ITIL V3 Service Transition book declares '***The Service Transition Team will soon become familiar with the need to change attitudes and the operation of converting culture. For them it is a routine task, holding no threat***' Perhaps that is why the current certification does not address this, since it is a routine task. However there is currently no 'practitioner' class to ensure that this is a routine task.*
  - *The question is, are the current ITIL training courses effective enough to enable us (you) to tackle the ABC issues you have identified?"*

Exercise 4: Task 1 – Adequacy of current training: (5 minutes)

Do the current ITIL training offerings help you to resolve the worst practices you have identified? Will they give us the organizational capabilities we need?

Number of answers
No they do not
Yes they do

Exercise 4: Task 2 – Additional training needs: (10 minutes)

What type of additional training is required? What do you need to learn in order to resolve the worst practices? Discuss and record the findings.

Type of training:

Learning needs:

Exercise 4: Task 3 – Selecting a training provider

When selecting an ITIL training provider ask them in the tender:

'How will you help us resolve <name the training needs and what needs to be learnt – taken from Task 2>'.

Ask to see the training course syllabus which shows this.

Exercise 4: Task 4 – Selecting a consulting or technology provider

When selecting any consulting partner (or tool provider) to help you with your ITIL program ask them:

'How will you resolve <ABC issues that need resolving – taken from Task xx>'.

Ask them for case studies and CV's which reference their ability to solve ABC issues.

Exercise 4 – Training needs

Teacher hints and tips for Exercise 4 - Tasks 2, 3 and 4

Task 2

- It is important that students attending ITIL training, especially managers, team leaders and process managers, are aware of the skills and capabilities they will need in order to ensure a successful deployment of ITIL. Use the findings of this task as input to the 'training' aspects of any 'service improvement program'.

Task 3 & 4

- It is important that organizations engaging with training, consulting or tool providers ensure that these 'partners' or 'suppliers' are capable of helping the organization to address any ABC worst practices, particularly, and especially if the results of Task 2 highlight in-house skills and capability issues.
- Use the captured worst practices from previous tasks as part of your selection criteria for partners and suppliers. Ensure they have demonstrated capabilities for helping you, not just a list of certified people.
- If the students each have a student manual then refer them to the 'personal notes and actions' for Task 2, 3 and 4 in their own manual. They can perform these actions back in their own organization.

Exercise 5 – Commitment and leadership

Exercise objectives

The objectives of this exercise are to:

- Identify whether there is commitment to making change happen. Commitment to adopting and deploying ITIL.
- Identify whether there is a recognized 'leadership' to ensure change does actually happen.
- Capture input that can be used for the 'leadership' exercise with a management team (see additional exercise cards).

Exercise background

As mentioned in earlier exercises, a recent Forrester report revealed that the most common reason for this type of project to fail is '52% resistance to change'. Lack of management commitment, lack of managers 'walking-the-talk' are examples of resistance.

The most popular cartoon chosen by organizations adopting ITIL is the 'commitment' cartoon which forms the basis of this exercise.

In a Gartner research note a couple of years ago it was announced:

*"...The most important IS capability that will determine success is 'Leadership'". The report went on to add: "....However, there are formidable challenges in the form of **internal leadership deficiencies** and senior executives who fail to recognize the need for strong leadership. Many IT leadership teams are poorly equipped to face the next two years."*

Exercise 5 – Commitment and leadership

Carry out the exercise

Exercise introduction

- Place the 5 of Diamonds card on the table.
- Read out the following to the team: *"Very often managers declare they are 'committed' to ITIL, experience reveals that they are sometimes the first ones to ignore or circumvent the procedures."*

Exercise 5: Task 1 – Commitment vote: (10 minutes)

Ask each individual if they agree or disagree with the following statement.

'Our managers are committed to making ITIL work'.

Record the answers on this form. Those who agree must give one example of behavior that describes what this 'commitment' looks like. Describe what management does that 'demonstrates' commitment. Those who disagree can also give an example of why they feel there is not enough 'commitment'.

Number of answers	
Agree	
Disagree	

Agree comments:

Disagree comments:

Exercise 5: Task 2 – What is leadership?: (10 minutes)

Read the following to the team and ask them to describe what 'leadership' is.

"There is a difference between management and leadership. In order for ITIL to work, managers must display leadership capabilities. What is leadership? Describe actions that show leadership?"

Leadership is:

Exercise 5 – Commitment and leadership

Teacher hints and tips for Exercise 5: Task 2

Let the teams try to describe what leadership is, then discuss the following:

- **Setting shared goals** – leaders ensure everybody is aware of the shared goals that are to be realized.
- **Motivate and inspire** – leaders try to motivate people to change, they inspire people to perform, they stimulate desirable behavior.
- **Walk the talk** – leaders 'lead by example', they show what new behavior should be.
- **Empower people** – leaders 'empower' and 'enable' people to change.
- **Remove barriers** – leaders remove barriers and obstacles that stand in the way of change, such as people refusing to change, tackling the ABC issues.

Exercise 5 – Commitment and leadership

Exercise 5: Task 3 – Demonstrating commitment & Leadership: (10 minutes)

Ask the team to look at the cards and choose those cards that demonstrate commitment and leadership.

- If you have already selected a number of cards in previous exercise, choose which of these cards can be solved by managers demonstrating 'leadership' and 'commitment' to making ITIL work.
- Alternatively, as a team chose the top five cards that managers should address in order to demonstrate 'leadership' and 'commitment' to making ITIL work.
- Write next to each card which manager(s) need to address these cards.

Exercise 5 – Commitment and leadership

Worksheet Task 3: Demonstrating commitment and leadership

Card:	Managers	

Exercise 5 – Commitment and leadership

Teacher hints and tips for Exercise 5: Task 3

- The results of this task can be used as input for a 'service improvement program'. It can be used to help create awareness at the management level, and it can also be used to select members of the improvement program.
- The results of this exercise can also be used as input for an exercise covering 'leadership' (see additional exercise cards). This exercise can be performed with management or leadership teams. The results of this exercise will hold a 'mirror' to managers and leaders, showing what the employees think and say about leadership.
- If the students each have a student manual then refer them to the 'personal notes and actions' for Task 3 in their own manual. They can perform these actions back in their own organization.

Additional exercise cards

The following are examples of other exercises you could perform using the cards. The exercises each look from a different perspective:

- Some are focused on a self assessment of your own weaknesses and strengths.
- Some are focused on a self assessment as you think how various other stakeholders would view you.
- Some are focused on how you view other stakeholders strengths and weaknesses.
- Some are focused toward management teams and to the business.

CEO

Goal: To force the teams to think from the perspective of the CEO, and to think what they would say about IT and why?

Set up: Play this with a group of IT managers. Give them a set of cards.

Explain: "Imagine, if we were to give these cards to the CEO and ask 'which of these cards is typical of YOUR IT organization?', which 3 would they choose and why?". Give examples that support your choice. Discuss if you KNOW this to be true. Discuss how you can find out what the CEO really sees as important improvements within the IT ABC.

This exercise is aimed at:

- Identifying what the CEO considers as ABC risks to the business.
- This exercise helps with a first step in resolving the card 5 of Clubs '**neither partner makes an effort to understand the other**' which scores high in polls and workshops.
- This will help identify key business and IT alignment worst practices such as:
  - IT not seen as an added value partner;
  - IT doesn't think it needs to understand the business to make a business case;
  - No understanding of business impact and priority;
  - IT doesn't measure its value contribution to strategy;
  - IT thinks it knows best.

Business unit assessment

Goal: To force the teams to think from the perspective of a specific Business Unit Manager or 'Customer', and to think what they would say about IT and why?

Set up: Split the group into teams. Give each team a set of cards. Place the Business Unit Manager (7 of Hearts) on the table, making introductions to the teams.

Explain: "Imagine, if we were to give these cards to the Business Unit Manager and ask 'which of these cards is typical of YOUR IT organization?', which 3 would they choose and why?"
Give examples that support your choice.
Let each team present 3.
Now discuss as one team what the overall top 3 would be?
Discuss "De we know enough about the business unit and their needs?"
Follow-up: confirm with the business and identify improvement initiatives.

This exercise is aimed at:

- Identifying what a specific business unit considers as ABC risks to their business.
- Identifying from an IT perspective the ABC issues that the business is guilty of.

- This exercise can help with a first step for IT to possibly address the worst practice 'No understanding of business impact and priority' and to discuss with the business the worst practice 'You DEMAND we GIVE IN'
- An additional task can be to let IT answer the following: "What do we see as the ABC worst practices displayed by the business unit?" Ask the business unit to also perform the task "Which ABC cards would IT choose to describe us?"
- The results of the above task can be discussed with the business, together with the consequences to both parties discussed.

Debate

Goal: To force people to debate the strengths and weaknesses of a selection of ABC cards in relation to their organization, by specifying actual examples to defend their position.

Set up: Split the team into two rows. (Like a debate). Pick a random card from the pack. (Or a number of cards that are relevant to your organization).
Pick 3 people to represent a jury of users or customers (or invite 3 real users).

Explain: The two teams are to take turns in debating the card.
One team must **agree** with the cards and provide real life examples that show it to be true.
One team must **disagree** and give real life examples that prove it to be wrong.
After 10 minutes let the jury vote:
'Does this worst practice apply to our organization? Yes or No?'

This exercise is aimed at:

- Identifying and agreeing both worst practices and best practices by debating real life experiences.
- Allowing users to agree or disagree with the findings.
- Allowing users to better understand how IT works and what they do for the business.
- Allowing IT to gain an insight into what users see and experience.
- Bringing IT and users together to discuss ABC issues.

You may consider selecting one of the worst practice cards that applies to the business, such as:

- 3 Diamonds: Poor business involvement in requirements specification and testing;
- 6 Diamonds: everything has the highest priority according to the users;
- 7 Hearts: Demand & Give. We demand and you give in.

Stakeholder Brainstorming

Goal: This is a brainstorming, free association exercise aimed at discovering, identifying and exploring possible ABC issues.

Set up: Split the Heart cards (Stakeholders) from the rest. Shuffle the Heart cards and shuffle the other 3 suits combined.
Place both sets face down on the table.

Explain: Select a card from the stakeholder pile and one from the other pile (combined clubs, diamonds and spades).
Discuss: Does this stakeholder display the Attitude, Behavior or Culture? Or is the stakeholder negatively effected by the Attitude, Behavior or Culture card? Or should the stakeholder play an active role in helping to remove this ABC issue?

This exercise is aimed at:

- Brainstorming, without having any specific perspective or preconceived expectations or defenses when attending this session.
- Identifying worst practices associated with various stakeholders, and/or stakeholders impacted by a worst practice, and/or stakeholders that need to play a role in resolving worst practices.

- This is a simple and effective way of performing a stakeholder analysis.
- The results can be sent to, and discussed with the various stakeholders.

Stakeholder SWOT

Goal: To identify a list of strengths and weaknesses for the various stakeholders of the IT organization

Set up: Pick a random stakeholder card. Give the Attitude, Behavior and Culture cards to a team.

Explain: Identify which 5 cards are the top 5 weaknesses or worst practices associated with this stakeholder.
Identify which 5 cards are in fact the strengths from this stakeholder. (They do the exact opposite).

This exercise is aimed at:

- Identifying the strengths and weaknesses of various stakeholders within the IT organization.
- Identifying weaknesses that need addressing for particular stakeholder groups.
- Identifying strengths that may represent desirable behavior or best practices that can be shared with other stakeholder groups.
- Identifying possible weaknesses that could cause IT improvement initiatives to fail.

- The results can now be discussed with that stakeholder group.
- The findings can be used as input to an ITSM improvement initiative.

Stakeholder perspective of YOUR department

Goal: To examine the IT organizations worst practice ABC issues from the perspective of all the stakeholders.

Set up: select a stakeholder card and place it face up on the table.

Explain: If we asked this stakeholder to choose the top 3 cards that represent YOUR IT department, or the top 3 cards that give them the most problems, which would they choose?
Explain why you chose and give a concrete example.
Now choose the stakeholders that are guilty of displaying the ABC cards that were chosen.

This exercise is aimed at:

- Forcing a team to view its performance from the perspective of all stakeholders in the supply chain.
- Helping a team to identify who is dependent upon them and who they are dependent upon.
- Identifying how the various stakeholders of an IT department or team view that department or team.

- This may help a team overcome a common complaint that IT is too internally focused. This allows them to think from the perspective of all stakeholders (both internal and external).
- This may also help a team address the issues of the Joker 'The Silo mentality'.
- This exercise is an 'outside-in' exercise that begins by looking at the external world and stakeholders.

 ## Self assessment

Goal: To rank the ABC cards according to impact and relevance to your organization, As seen by various teams or groups.

Set up: Invite members from a team or department. Give them a set of cards.

Explain: Ask them to work and discuss as a team. Ask them to put each suit in order of the most important issue to be addressed from their team or department perspective. For the top 3 ABC cards ask them to pick the relevant stakeholder card, identifying the stakeholder that causes them the most pain. Write these up and discuss with the team leader how these can best be addressed together with the stakeholders.

This exercise is aimed at:

- Allowing a specific team or department to assess the worst practices that impact their team performance.
- Allowing teams to prioritize these based upon the impact to their work.
- Allowing teams to identify specific stakeholders that are causing the team the most pain.
- Enabling team leaders to identify issues that they need to discuss with other stakeholder groups.

- This helps teams to be less internally focused and can assist in breaking down the Joker card 'The Silo mentality'.
- This is an 'inside-out' exercise that begins by looking at the internal view as experienced by the team, and sees the outside world as causes of pain and suffering.

Own strengths

Goal: To help identify a teams blind spots and unrecognized issues.

Set up: Give a set of cards to a team.

Explain: Ask the team to choose the top 3 A, B and C cards that are the LEAST relevant to the team. In other words the team displays 'desirable behavior' in these areas.
Ask the team to pick 2 stakeholder cards to check this.
Follow-up: Explain your choices to these 2 stakeholders and ask if they agree.
Now ask the stakeholders to look at the ABC cards and choose 3 that they would like to see improved within your team or department.

This exercise is aimed at:

- Identifying what a team sees as desirable behavior.
- Identifying what a team sees as its own strengths.
- Allowing a team to check this perception against other stakeholders.
- Allowing stakeholders to give feedback to the team on the team's strengths and the improvements needed.

- The team can then discuss the findings and identify what desirable and undesirable behavior is, and agree what changes they may need to make as a team.
- This is an 'inside-out' exercise that begins by looking at how a team perceives its own strengths'. This can then be checked with stakeholders to get an 'outside-in' view and a reality check.
- This can be matched against the aims and goals of an improvement program.

 ## Managers

Goal: To raise management team awareness for ABC within their organization and to discuss the findings in relation to possible impact and consequences.

Set up: Give each manager a set of cards, or shuffle the cards and divide them over the management team.

Explain: Ask each management team member to choose 1 A card, 1 B card and 1 C card from their cards that is the most relevant for their organization.
Let each manager explain their choice.
Put all the chosen cards on the table and rank as a management team which A,B and C card creates the most pain in the organization. Identify which stakeholders are guilty of this.
As a team, discuss: "Can we afford to do nothing about this or do we need to take action to resolve this?"
"If we do nothing what will be the consequences?" Think in terms of business risks and business value.

This exercise is aimed at:

- Raising awareness for ABC within a management team.
- Allowing managers to identify, discuss and agree key ABC issues affecting their organization, the impact and consequences of these issues and who is causing them.
- Allowing managers to identify if adequate measures have already been taken for resolving the ABC issues.

- This exercise can help to make managers aware of ABC worst practices and how these may have a negative impact upon a planned or current improvement initiative.

Leadership

Goal: To let the management team assess its leadership, as they perceive it.

Set up: Give a management team the following cards: 9 & 10 of Clubs, 5 of Diamonds, 3 of Spades, 5 of Spades, 9 of Spades, King of Spades.

Explain: If we gave these cards to the employees which ones would they take and pin up on the notice board saying that is our management.
Discuss why. Describe example situations that would cause them to say that.
Which ones are you definitely not guilty of?
Follow-up: 360 degree feedback. Ask somebody to select an anonymous group to discuss and give feedback on your choices with case examples.
Discuss as a management team what you will do about this? And if you do nothing what may be the impact?

This exercise is aimed at:

- Identifying what the management team think about their own performance and how they feel they are viewed by their employees.
- Identifying if the management team feel they are committed to change programs and enabling them to identify whether this is felt by the employees.

- Leadership and commitment are seen as two key success and fail factors for ITSM improvement initiatives. Poor leadership and lack of real commitment and 'walking-the-talk' are reasons for resistance. 52% of ITSM improvement projects that fail, do so because of 'resistance'.
- Output from other exercises and team sessions can be used as input for this session, to hold a 'mirror' up to the managers' own attitudes and behavior that they may not be aware of.

 ## Giving the 'Yellow' card

Goal: To help remind people of, and confront people with undesirable behaviour.

Set up: Give a set of already agreed worst practice cards to each employee.

Explain: Whenever you see anybody displaying one of these worst practices take the card out of your pocket and hold it up like a referee holding up a `yellow card´ and say ´you have been booked´. Discuss why you held the card up and see if the other person agrees.

This exercise is aimed at:

- Continually confronting people with ABC worst practices and undesirable behavior.

- This can be done after other exercises have already been performed.
- This can be done when the IT organization, department or team has already agreed to what undesirable behavior they want to get rid of.
- This can help remind and reinforce the commitment to remove worst practices and undesirable behavior.
- The cards that are to be eliminated can be given to all employees so that ANYBODY can show the Yellow card if they see undesirable behavior.

Brainstorming fun

Goal: To brainstorm and identify ABC issues, relationships and dependencies.

Set up: Play a normal card game with the cards, such as Poker or Black Jack.

Explain: Let the person who wins a hand of cards explain his winning hand in relation to ABC behaviour in your organization. Do you display these worst practices or not. If there is a 'stakeholder' card in the hand what is the relationship with the other cards. Is the 'stakeholder' guilty of one of the ABC cards problems? Or is the 'stakeholder' responsible for resolving one of the ABC card issues. Discuss your findings.

This exercise is aimed at:

- Team building and having fun. Teams can actually 'play card games' using the cards.
- Brainstorming, using the results of the winning card games to identify ABC cards that are relevant to the organization.

 Real-life cases - support

Goal: To use real life cases to determine which ABC aspects underpin this.

Set up: Each participant writes on a piece of paper a real 'worst practice' situation they have experienced.
e.g. 'I work on the Help Desk; yesterday the server was out and nobody told us. The users called up to ask what was happening, we asked 2nd line support and they sent us away without any information we could give to the users. We told our manager who said he would ensure this didn't happen again, but nothing was ever said or done.'

Explain: Read the case to the team and ask each person to select the ABC cards that underpin this situation.

This exercise is aimed at:

- Allowing team members to write down and discuss real life worst practices.
- Identifying which ABC worst practice cards underpin these worst practices, and which stakeholders are guilty of these.

- This allows the team to describe real life situations that are causing them pain, and use these to analyze the underlying causes that are in need of addressing.

Real life cases - Change

Goal: To use real life cases to determine which ABC aspects underpin this.

Set up: Each participant writes on a piece of paper a real situation, without any positive or negative descriptions.
e.g. 'The user calls the Help Desk to request information about a change. When will it be scheduled, will it be on time.
Now shuffle the cards and select an ABC card.

Explain: If this ABC card applies to us what type of reaction would we give to the user request above? Do we behave like this?

This exercise is aimed at:

- Allowing team members to write down and discuss real life working situations and identify how the organization responds to these.
- Identifying how the team responds or deals with the real life situations that have been written down.

Implementation

Goal: To identify ABC issues in making ITSM improvements or 'implementing' ITIL.

Set up: Take the following cards our of the set and place them on the table.
6,7,9, King and Ace of Clubs,
4,8, Queen and King of Spades
5,7,8,10 and Ace of Diamonds
Get a team of managers, or ITSM improvement managers, or process managers or team leaders together.

Explain: Which of these cards do we think describes our approach to ITSM improvements? What is the impact of this? What counter measures can we include in the ITSM improvement initiative to reduce these implementation risks.

This exercise is aimed at:

- Identifying current or perceived ABC issues that may delay or derail an ITSM improvement initiative.
- Allowing participants to explain real life situations that they see/have seen in relation to other improvement initiatives.
- Identifying what the impact can be in terms of delay, lack of buy-in, lack of commitment, increased effort or increased resistance.

- The results can be fed into an improvement initiative to ensure adequate communication, awareness, involvement and leadership in order to mitigate the implementation risks.

Appendix A:
Global Results

The figures below represent the global results of the ABC worst practice round table sessions held so far (up until publication date of this guide). These were 30 to 45 minute sessions held at several international locations. During these sessions the 'customer and user focused' exercise was performed.

The first set of figures identifies the top three cards chosen in each suit. Table 1 represents the most commonly chosen worst practice cards. The second table, Table 2, identifies the 'impact' of the worst practices as identified in an online survey and gathered from the round table sessions.

GamingWorks would like to regularly update and publish these global findings. In order to do this we need your input. If you perform the 'customer and user focused' exercise please send use the results of task 2 so that we can add them to our existing results.

The **figures below** represent the **consolidated results** of the ABC workshops held so far in a number of different countries. These figures are based upon more than 300 attendees.

Attitude
• No understanding of business impact and priority (36)
• IT thinks it doesn't need to understand the business to make a business case (17)
• ITIL never work here (15)

Behavior
• Throwing ITIL solutions over the wall and hoping people will follow them (27)
• Everything has the highest priority according to the users (27)
• Process managers without authority (26)

Culture
• Not my responsibility (41)
• Internally focused (35)
• Blame culture (28)

Hearts
- Project manager. Of course we will finish on time and within budget! (14)
- The Quality manager. Waiting for the IT organization to improve! (12)
- Business manager. Demand & Give. I demand and you give in! (11)

What are the top 10 worst practices?

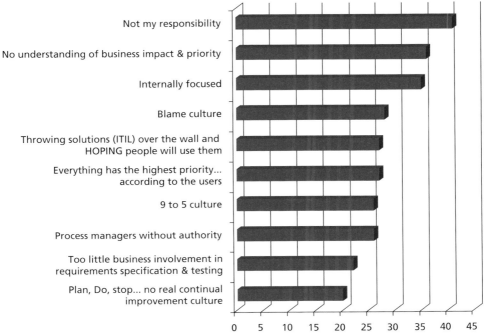

Table 1

These are the results of the 'impact' on the business as taken from an online survey conducted in the Netherlands and the results of the round table sessions gathered so far.

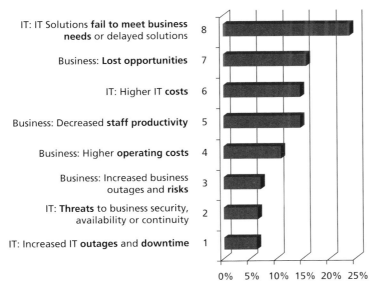

Table 2

Appendix B:
Example 'Attitude' and 'Behavior' Change Using the Cards

The following is a short example of how the card exercises helped to change the attitude and behavior of a manager. I have chosen this example as it relates to one of the top three globally recognized worst practices in the ABC of ICT card set.

Case:

Here is a small case of using the ABC cards to identify that the Queen of Clubs 'No understanding of business impact and priority' was an issue in the company. I used the cards in an itSMF conference workshop. We started the session by having people put the 2 of Clubs on the table:

> ITSM best practice trainer teaching people about ITIL. "ITIL uses the terms customers and users, what terms do you use?"
>
> The technoids in the class reply "Dorks!"

People then voted on the statement: "We are not customer focused enough in IT."

- In the itSMF website vote **89%** agreed with the statement and gave examples of behavior that needed changing, many of them directly related to the ABC cards.
- At the itSMF best practice conference **86%** agreed.
- The itSMF Academy workshop scored considerably lower. Only **75%** agreed with the statement.

I walked around the teams to get a feel of their 'attitude'. This is what I saw and experienced:

- By one table there was 'irritation', and the 'crossed-arm', 'head shaking' negative body language, implying that it was a mistake attending this session.
- "So you obviously don't agree?" I asked.
- "Now…yeah. Listen, **of course we are customer focused! We are IT managers at this table and we talk to customers all the time.** If you talk about the support teams and the techies

then you are right....what do you want us to vote? Of course we can make your figures look high!?"

- "Vote as you perceive it", I said. "The idea is to recognize worst practices that need fixing..... you obviously don't have any.......**as managers.**"
- Their attitude was WE don't need to change. WE have no worst practice BEHAVIOR.

As part of the next task we put the 'User' card on the table. The task was:

"Imagine the end-users or customers are sitting here at the table and we give them the pack of worst practice cards. We then ask them to select three cards that apply to your organization; which cards would they choose?"

Each participant chose three cards.

The aim of this task was at force them to think from a different perspective, try to take time out from the daily operation to think from the perspective of another stakeholder. The stakeholder that we provide IT services for, in fact!

The next task was to discuss all the cards chosen and select, as a team, the top three. *The interesting aspect now was how to choose a team top three.* Should we choose the cards that were chosen the most? I told them to choose using the following criteria, related to ITIL V3 Service Strategy and 'value'. Value talks about 'fit for use' and 'fit for purpose'.

"Look at each card and discuss the consequences to the business. Think in terms of wasted money, lost revenue, delayed projects, down-time and non-availability of critical systems, solutions that fail to deliver business value". This created a range of new discussions and new insights.

The teams were finally finished. I asked them all, including the team of 'customer focused' managers to present their findings. I call this team the A-Team for obvious reasons, heroic champions capable of aligning business and IT single-handedly.

These were the results:

- The A-team (as well as three other teams) chose the card the Queen of Clubs 'No understanding of business impact and priority' as the top recognized worst practice.
- Example behavior was:
  - the business won't invite us to discuss business needs, we are too late in the process;
  - we try to tell the business but they won't listen;
  - we allocate resources and start a project portfolio and then find they are no longer important;
  - we have business users declaring that the solutions don't meet their needs.
- Example consequences were:
  - failure to solve 'real' business problems;
  - delays in business projects;
  - lost business opportunities and business revenue;
  - not enough testing, causing downtime and additional changes;

- unpredictable services and project performance;
- increased costs;
- business dissatisfaction
- IT frustration.

I then asked the team "Is this an acceptable business risk?"

The answer was "NO!"

Now the 64 million dollar question. "Now that you recognize that this is what you, as an IT organization, do and that it is an unacceptable business risk, IS THERE ANYBODY ACCOUNTABLE IN YOUR (IT) ORGANIZATION FOR RESOLVING THIS?"………

There was a moment of silence…. "No"

"So let me just summarize then, to see if I understand. YOU IT managers are customer focused enough…..however, you accept that your current behavior causes unacceptable business risks? And you also accept that you don't need to do anything to ensure that this business issue is resolved….is this an example of being customer focused enough?"

The vote was now 100% at the A-Team. "We are not customer focused enough." "So what are you going to do now?" I asked.

"We are going to perform this exercise in our organization…..more people need to be confronted with the consequences of our attitude and behavior"

Appendix C:
Example Follow-up to Address a Worst Practice

The following case is an example of how an intervention can be made to resolve a worst practice. We have chosen this card and example because a Forrestor report revealed that the key reason for ITIL implementations struggling is 'resistance to change'. The need to get buy-in is a crucial success factor. This intervention was done as a result of the card 'ITIL Never work here' being selected by a manager. "This is what we see" he said. "Many people have bought in to ITIL, but a hardcore of people, who are influential, still openly moan and criticize. They are influencing others and creating a bad feeling."

Case: Use of a business simulation to create buy-in

There are many business simulations on the market. They are all good, they all help to overcome resistance and gain buy-in. A Forrestor report stated:

ITIL simulators demonstrate the value of process models, September 1, 2006

'These tools effectively demonstrate to senior management the advantages of such process models (ITIL). The result: better management buy-in for an IT service management (ITSM) project and its benefits and an implementation team with a better understanding of the value of the end state of the initiative.'

Research result into the question:
"What negative elements were encountered during implementation?"
The highest scoring response was "Internal resistance to change - 52%".

"Considering the enormity of change that an ITIL project may entail, spending the day required by such simulators should pay back many times over with the creation of a cohesive team with a greater understanding of the components, interrelationships and vision that are required to successfully transform an IT organization."

In this example we are referring to the use of the Simulation Apollo 13 to help resolve the worst practice.

Example:

Apollo 13 was used as an instrument to help create awareness of the benefits of process working, and at the same time capture input for a service improvement initiative. Capturing improvement initiatives from the shop-floor helped 'empower' the employees; at the same time it was played with teams made up of different departments in order to break down the 'silo' mentality that existed. At the start of an Apollo 13 simulation we were told that this particular group was filled with 'resisters', "these people will not accept it…", "these people will work against you." This was the last session and was seen as the session of 'no hopers'.

We did an introductory round. "What do you expect from this training?"

"I expect this will be a waste of time!"
"… I could be doing something more useful"
"… I do not believe in this process stuff…"

When asked to clarify, it came down to 'too much unnecessary registration and bureaucracy that nobody needs…'

"We don't have the time to explain or hand-over…."
"It will just give me MORE work and more people telling us what to do…"

It was clear this resistance was related to time pressures, workload and not believing that processes could help in any way.

We played Apollo. The initial round was a disaster. There was stress, frustration, anger and a general belief of "see, we told you that processes were a waste of time." The sponsor for the workshop was getting worried. We had made the resistors even angrier and they had even more reason to believe they were right.

The interventions in the game, thought up by the resistors themselves, were:

- get rid of the annoying repeat work that was wasting their time;
- agree a priority mechanism to help everybody decide what work should be done first;
- agree an escalation mechanism so that somebody else could make a call on priority when there was a conflict about what to do next;
- agree to give each other the right information to enable everyone to do what they need to do;
- agree to give each other feedback when things are not working as agreed.

We tested their new procedures, process design and agreements. The next round went much smoother. They achieved their goals and targets. We asked them "How does it feel?"

"Smoother, easier, less stress, more time to pick up the difficult projects, more ability to plan."
"How come?" we asked.

They concluded that it was because they had agreed their own procedures, they had all done what they had agreed and promised, they had handed over some of the workload to other people. They had, in fact, done all of the things they were being asked to do but now they were able to experience the difference this made to their own tasks.

We reflected back on what had happened and how we had listened to their underlying concerns, and we tried to show them how these could be solved by doing the very thing they were resisting.

The reflection comments were:

"...I didn't realize it could make our lives easier.."
"...this stuff can work, I must admit I am surprised. I will tell my team we need to get involved and make sure the process design project involves us so we can ensure the right things are done..."